Eilean Donan Castle

# Timeless Landscapes

*by Chris Banks*

Published by Arc Publishing and Print
166 Knowle Lane
Sheffield
S11 9SJ

Telephone 07809 172872

# Contents

## Acknowledgements

Many thanks to:

Calum Mackinnon - for his kindness in taking us out on his fishing boat to photograph the white tail sea eagle.

Kirsty Robinson - for her sketch "Blaven Cow".

Sir Patrick Moore - for his inspiration in igniting a passion for astronomy when I was a young boy and his kindness on a recent visit.

Chris Keeling - for the opportunity to publish my first book.


This book is dedicated to my wife June for her unconditional love and never ending support.

# Introduction:

During the sixties and seventies many families, including mine, spent their holidays in caravans close to Skegness and Mablethorpe. At that time we had an old Ford Anglia and to do a hundred and sixty mile round trip without a puncture or a breakdown, was in itself quite an achievement. Loading such a small car with everything but the kitchen sink was impossible, so the bulk of it ended up on the roof, covered with plastic sheeting and held together with a piece of old washing line.

Months before the holiday my brother and I collected bags of copper and silver coins saved from the pocket money given to us by our parents, aunts and uncles.

We even returned empty bottles back to the local off-license for the few pennies refund.
This was to fuel our fascination with slot machines.
On one occasion I recall we both disappeared to the arcade across from the caravan site with a small bag of copper, and came back a short time later with our trousers almost around our ankles with the weight of coins in our pockets.

Something had gone wrong with the horse-racing machine and we were winning every time we placed a bet. It was quite a while before the arcade owners realised what was happening and by then we had made a quick escape with our bulging small fortune in old pennies.

Those holidays on the east coast also helped kindle my early passion for astronomy. From my caravan bed I would look out through the window and stare up at the night sky. It was darker but much clearer than back home in Sheffield where pollution from the orange street lights marred my view of the sky. My parents then bought me a pair of binoculars. The first direction I pointed them was straight up at the night sky. That lit the fuse and the quest was on to see objects in more detail. One birthday I received a small refracting telescope, which gave an extra boost in magnification. I could now see the rings of Saturn, the moons and cloud bands of Jupiter and close details of the craters and seas of the Moon. My interest in Astronomy continued to grow and after starting my first job I saved up and acquired a special telescope from America with an eight inch aperture. It was of compact design and electronically driven which enabled me to track celestial objects. The beauty of such a telescope is that a camera can be attached to photograph the images. This was when my love of photography began.

At present I live with my wife June on the outskirts of the Peak district. I have grown up knowing this area and enjoy walking and nature watching whenever possible. There are many good walks but one that stands out from the rest is Kinder Scout, a small mountain that is well worth doing. But a word of warning - be prepared for the cheeky sheep which, when you stop for lunch, will try to get into your rucksack, virtually sitting in your lap, wanting to share your sandwich.

My love for Scotland started on a sad note in the early eighties. My father had been diagnosed with cancer and he wanted us all to have a holiday at North Berwick which was to include a game of golf. I began playing golf at a young age with a set of old clubs and joined the local golf club where my father played. I went there most Saturdays and won various competitions reaching a handicap of seven.

I played particularly well on this strange course in Scotland. I hit so many greens and sunk so many putts that by the end of the round I had had only dropped about four shots to par. There was a look of total disbelief on my fathers face. Sadly this turned out to be our last game together and now I play golf very rarely because, to me, the game will never be the same again.

North Berwick on the east coast of Scotland is a lovely place with views of the bass rock out to sea in the distance, which is home to a very large colony of Gannets. One evening after a walk with my wife we called at the local fish and chip shop and ordered pie and chips. I was totally astonished when the lady serving us proceeded to put the pie in a basket and fry it in the chip fat. We both gave each other a blank look and left the shop with our meals. It actually tasted fantastic but goodness only knows how many calories it contained.

Another expedition over the Scottish border was to be a long weekend to Edinburgh with our very close friends Steve and Jane. This included a journey up to Crieff incorporating a visit to the Glen Turret distillery. We proceeded up the glen to Loch Turrett, which we all agreed was stunning, igniting a desire to see more of this beautiful area.

The love of the Highlands and Islands continued with holidays in Orkney, Islay, Jura and even little Gigha. On the mainland we visited Ullapool which to me has the feel of an island. Moving further up the north west coast we reached Lochinver which is surrounded by a wild emptiness sprinkled with isolated mountains. Being keen walkers, this area proved to be irresistible.

Suilven

Looking at these mountains from a distance they appear to be impossible to climb - especially Suilven and Stac Pollaidh. However, on closer inspection, they usually have well designed routes up them. One of my favourites is Quinag which although not a Munro
(a Scottish mountain over three thousand feet) has a fine ridge walk and fantastic views of the Lochinver area. Looking down from the summit the road looks like a long piece of string weaving its way between small lochs and lochens.

Having thoroughly enjoyed this area of the Scottish Mainland, in my book I will mainly concentrate on the Isles of Skye and Mull. I am not setting out to give you a detailed guide to these islands involving facts and figures. I just want you to have a brief glimpse, a taster if you like, of the natural beauty of these isles.

Visiting these places over the years has affected me deeply in many ways.
I would like to share these memories with you. After trying to paint without great success, I feel that it is through my photography I am better able to express my feelings for this lovely part of the world.

Quinag Ridge

View from the Summit of Quinag

# Isle of skye

## Something Special

It is our love for walking and nature, combined with photography, which draws us to the far north of Scotland for our holidays.

After reading many walking magazines and books about the Isle of Skye, it was only a matter of time before we made the long journey north which began a long love affair with this Island. Skye can be reached in three ways by car. In the summer months there are the ferries from Mallaig to Armardale, and from Glenelg to Kylerhea. But our crossing has always been over the Skye Bridge. The first time across started a little ritual - to play a piece of music. We both enjoy Scottish/ Celtic music and one of our favourite bands is Runrig. The track we play is the one called "Morning Sunrise". It never fails to bring a lump in the throat and a small tear in the eye. Which is the opposite to when we leave the island in complete silence.

Lower Breakish

We turn right after the bridge and after a few miles we reach Broadford which is probably the second most populated town after the capital, Portree. Broadford offers a mixture of craft shops, visitor attractions and wildlife.

The supermarket is in a stunning location looking out over Broadford Bay which even on a dull day has a serene quality. It is an ideal place to see many wading birds and ducks. There are not many supermarkets where you can watch a school of dolphins playing and feeding in the bay whilst loading up the car with shopping.

Travelling north from Broadford the road snakes it way around the Lochs and over the mountains all the while giving magnificent views of Skye's timeless landscape.

Dropping down the far side of the mountains you pass through Sconser where you can catch the car ferry to Skye's near neighbour Raasay .
A few winding miles later you turn the final bend to arrive at Sligachan.
I remember the very first time we did this journey and the Cuillin Mountains came in to view. It was an unbelievable sight. They could have almost come straight out of Tolkien's 'Lord of the Rings'.

Cuillin Mountains

Having read plenty of books on the Cuillin I was eager to explore. The Sligachan view of the peaks as with the view from Glen Brittle is very deceptive as there is a good walk before you start to climb. One thing you notice as you move closer to your goal is the silence. Only the breeze and the occasional bird call can be heard, giving your ears something to focus on.

Eventually you come face to face with the Cuillin in an intimidating rocky amphitheatre.

The two so called easier walks are Bruach na Frithe and Blaven. Blaven is the only Cuillin peak which is separated from the main ridge. They still require a fair level of fitness as you will be walking for six or seven hours. You also need a good head for heights. There is no knife edge exposure but caution is required on the loose scree.

Our second day trip involved taking the car over because we wanted to explore more of the island. The drive from our base on Skye was with the hope of having good weather. Still the forecast was favourable. Our first stop was to climb Duncaan, a small peak with the appearance from a distance, of the devils tower in the 'Close Encounters' film. It is the highest part of Raasay at 443 metres. We were hoping for brilliant views and we were not disappointed. The walk was not hard, just a steady incline. With each stop the views changed as more and more of the water surrounding Raasay came into view. The outlook towards Skye was breathtaking with low mist shortly to be replaced with blue skies. We began to think that this could be a very special day.

After about a mile we reached a level area with a small lochen looking directly ahead to Duncaan. The path then dropped steeply over a few hundred feet, leading into a small ravine filled by a big lochan. Everything was so still. The only sound was of the peaty water lapping on to a small beach. The silence was overwhelming.

We are now at the base of Duncaan and we could see the path winding around the rocky peak like a helter skelter. Twenty minutes later we were on a plateau. The cloud and mist had lifted and from our vantage point, at the summit, most of Raasay could be seen stretching out before us.

After touching the obligatory trig point, the silence was broken by a small fishing boat heading out to sea. It was barely visible, apart from a small wake in the bluest of blue waters giving near perfect mirror image of the sky. It was time for lunch or should I say 'summit nic'. After a short while we were joined at the summit by two people and we were no longer 'kings of the castle'.

We headed further up the island where we stopped to talk to a local man who was stacking peat for drying. He told us that his style was similar to that used in the Western Isles. It was noticeably different to what we had seen previously on Skye.

All too soon another Raasay day has come to an end. I would just like to finish by saying that anybody visiting Skye should put one day aside to explore this close, quiet, rugged neighbour. I am sure that it would be a day that would live long in the memory.

Yours truly at the summit

# Blaven and the Cows

One of my favourite Cuillin mountain tops is "Blaven" or Bla Bheinn. (In Gaelic)
This mountain summit has a spectacular panorama with a loch, sea views and the rest of the main Cuillin range.
To get the best views of Blaven, go through the small township of Torrin and as you drive round the far side of Loch Slappin you will find a purpose built car park.

## Cuillin

Cuillin Mountains jagged and torn

Cuillin Mountains primordial born

Awesome nature laid bare to see

With dark rock towers and hated scree

Hidden corries silent and still

Quickening heartbeat, the ridge, the thrill

The last few steps awkward and steep

Conquered fears with views to weep

Cuillin Mountains of volcanic mother

Cuillin Mountains standing like no other

———

Chris Banks

This walk to the base of Blaven is shorter than any other Cuillin walk, allowing you to loosen up in preparation for the steeper sections to come. The path climbs slowly following the river which feeds in to the loch. There are numerous hidden gullies and small waterfalls, creating crystal clear pools which appear turquoise green due to the colour of the pebbles that lie beneath.

Occasionally over the sound of rushing water, we could hear the distinctive

Stonechat

call of a stone chat. It is pretty little bird, which makes a sound similar to that of someone trying to light a fire with two flints.

Journey up Blaven

34

Eventually you come to a point where you cross the river and are faced with a steep section which climbs up into the Corrie Uaigneich. I remember one year, from this point looking across and seeing a herd of deer disappearing over the opposite hill. Their white rumps bounced up and down, a great spectacle and a real bonus to the walk.

View from the top of Blaven

On reaching the Corrie there is a lochen on your left and an intimidating scree slope straight ahead. The normally easier route takes you sharp right where you head for the skyline. The final part of this Blaven walk is the steepest but still requires a couple of small scrambles to reach the summit. Recently on this walk (at approximately two thousand feet) we came across a Ring Ouzel, a summer visitor to our shores. The final few feet to the summit is a gentle stroll. However the anticipation begins to grow as you approach the trig point, which depending on how you feel could be hugged, kissed, or just given a gentle pat.

Ring Ouzel

The Summit
and Trig point

36

You need a nice clear day for your walk to take in the full 360 degree panorama.

Spread out in front of you is the main Cuillin ridge.

To the left the views open out with seascapes dotted with islands. To the right of the ridge you see Skye's near neighbour the Isle of Raasay laid out before you in all its low rugged splendour.

Time on the summit of mountains appears to pass quickly and what seems to be fifteen or twenty minutes is in fact an hour. After all the effort in reaching the top, combined with breathtaking views, there is a always a reluctance to leave.

The mountain journey is still only half completed with the downhill leg still to come. Caution, at this point is always advised as tiredness sets in as your legs become shock absorbers.

Remember no mountain climb is ever completed until you are safe and well back at the start.

After completing our walk up the mountain, which had left us tired and pretty exhausted, we began the drive back. Just as we left Torrin we approached a cattle grid, with two cows standing side by side, staring down at it as if in conversation. The scene had the look of a cartoon sketch about it. Then one of them, as if being egged on by the other, stepped out in front of the car, causing us to stop. It seemed to be acting like a bovine border guard. For a few moments she stared at us as if daring us to move, then she began coming towards us. But unfortunately for the cow, she had to cross the grid to get to us and within the first couple of strides, one of her front legs dropped into the grid. This was all we needed after a long days walk. I got out of the car and tried to push the cow backwards out of the grid. But after a brief struggle, she managed to get her back legs stuck as well. Now what? I carried on pushing, shoving and coaxing, until eventually, after a lot of determination, a couple of sore shoulders and a lot of sweat, plus luck, the cow became free. I had to smile as I watched her trot off to carry on her conversation with her friend as if nothing had happened. And here was I, left bent over covered in sweat and panting for all I was worth. A few cars had backed up in both directions by this time. Before getting back into my car, I grinned and gave them all a bow.

Drawing by
Kirsty Robinson

# Christmas on Skye

In December 2006, for the first time, we had Christmas on the Isle of Skye. It was something that we had thought about for a long time but never done. We had  doubts about the weather and short days, but we put all this to one side and went for it. There was slight trepidation as we approached the bridge, knowing that it is not called the Misty Isle of Skye for nothing. But to our surprise the sun shone through broken cloud and we had a lovely view of the mountains in winter.

# Otters

Special things can happen on these islands, if you are lucky and are prepared for an early start to the day.
It was the last morning of our memorable stay on Skye.
We were awake early and the weather was perfect - early sunshine and not a cloud in the sky. It was just after six o'clock so before having breakfast we decided to have one more look around the harbour for our furry friends.
It was warm, calm and quiet with no one around.

Armed with camera and binoculars we looked around the harbour and out into the loch on the chance of seeing something special. After about half an hour we were reluctant to drag ourselves away for breakfast. I decided to walk down to the waters edge on the slipway for one last look, and saw through the binoculars a mum otter and two cubs swimming on the far side of the harbour.

I could hardly contain my excitement and tried to get my wife's attention, without attracting the otters. It worked and we both watched this family for about twenty minutes. Her cubs were diving and feeding, plus bouts of wrestling and throwing seaweed in the air. However they were still too far away to get any decent photographs. Then, I thought all my birthdays had come at once when the otters changed direction and came swimming towards us.

We were rooted to the spot, hardly breathing and hoping they would not get spooked.

I gingerly began to take some photos, trying at the same time to keep one eye on where they were heading. They went directly under the slipway and out into the loch. They hugged the shoreline all the way - just being utterly otterly! Finally they disappeared from view.

I have had some good otter encounters but so far this one has been the best... but you just never know!

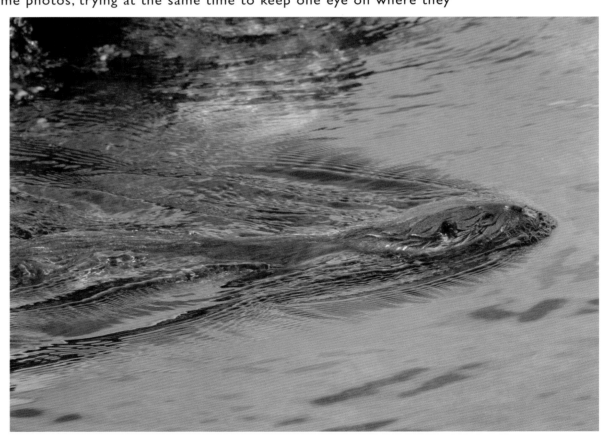

Wildlife - watching in these wild and beautiful places just seems a natural thing to do. It is important, however, that you do not get discouraged, as it is not every trip that brings success. A bit of luck and a lot of patience is needed in this fast moving world.

Give yourself time to slow down and learn to heighten your senses and just train your eye to look a little more closely at what might seem to be a clump of seaweed on the shore. Using your binoculars, you may find that there is an otter asleep in the seaweed, as its fur when dry, blends perfectly.

When birds of prey, like the majestic Sea Eagle are not flying they like to perch on their favourite spots, maybe the same branch in a tree or on rocks. Careful observation is required, along with a little local knowledge. It is always helpful when people with simular interests are prepared to share their experiences.

The landscape and its moods can also present opportunities especially if you visit around the longest day in June, because at these latitudes on the Islands it never gets really dark even at midnight. So after your evening meal take yourself out for a small walk or a leisurely drive and catch the sunset.
I remember one June evening driving down the Glen Brittle road about ten in the evening to photograph the Cuillin mountains at sunset. I was not disappointed as conditions were perfect with clear skies right down to sea level. The sun at this time sets at the end of Loch Harport slowly turning the normally black Cuillin first to yellow, then through orange, and finally to a lovely dark red, which looked like Skye's version of Ayers Rock in Australia.
As soon as the sun dips below the horizon the Cuillin, take on their usually dark, menacing, foreboding appearance.

Cuillin Mountains - June evening

# A Perfect Present

Having experienced Christmas on Skye once before the decision to return for another was not a hard one. It is a bit of a gamble with the weather but one that it well worth taking. I am generally not much of a humbug but I feel Christmas has lost a lot of the values which I enjoyed as a small boy. Christmas decorations appear in the shops in September and the television starts pumping out advertisements for toys and gifts which would cost a small fortune. I feel that most of this is totally unnecessary.

So the great escape was on, the only draw back being the ten hour drive and the lack of daylight at this time of the year making for a tiring journey. However all of this is forgotten when you cross on to the island and a sense of calm and anticipation sets in.

View from Portnalong Harbour

One of the most noticeable differences about Skye at this time of the year is the light which provides an extra dimension in your photographs, making ordinary views more exciting. The golden glows of the landscape are due to the browny orange colour of the grass and heather which, even on the most gloomy of days, gives a warming appearance totally opposite from the greens of summer.

The island is quiet with few visitors at this time of the year, but there are always the hardy climbers that take on the Cuillin mountains which are even more of a challenge in their winter mantle. There is a feeling that the whole area is in hibernation, resting and waiting for the onslaught of walkers and climbers who come in the tourist season for the natural beauty of the place and its well stocked larder of native wildlife.

This Christmas week is also a time to catch up with old acquaintances, human as well as animal. Staying not far from Portnalong harbour it was the obvious choice for our first port of call. We met our friend Calum Mackinnon, the fisherman who had earlier in the year very kindly taken us out on the loch to see the White Tail Sea Eagle which gave me the opportunity to photograph these magnificent birds. We promised him a nice bottle of Malt for his kindness, which we passed to him with our gratitude.

He mentioned to us the otters, which he had seen about three weeks earlier were still together as a family group consisting of mum and two cubs. The same family I had photographed earlier in June and even then the cubs appeared to be nearly full grown.

It was not until Christmas day that we spotted an otter. We had bought a lovely piece of pork for our Christmas dinner making a change from the regular turkey.
Leaving the joint in the oven to cook nice and slowly we set off for the harbour. After about one hour of intense scouting we found our otter fishing in the far side of the bay.

She was working her way round the edge of the shore diving in amongst the seaweed for small fish. Now came a change of clothes the speed of which superman would have been proud. On with the camouflage jacket, dark hat and gloves, in a vane attempt to mask the typical human outline. My wife would keep the otter under surveillance through her binoculars and guide me into position using walkie talkies, a great piece of equipment for this type of activity, but don't forget to turn them off when you get close. The greatest thing ever

is to witness these otters doing otterly things in their natural surroundings.
As a break from fishing they occasionally come out the water to eat a crab or to do some fur maintenance ensuring that their coat keeps it waterproof properties.

Trying to get close is not easy but I work my way along the shoreline crouching behind any rocks that are available, at the same time waiting for the familiar site of an otter diving under the waves. Her long tail whips over as she submerges and only at this point do I move a little closer trying to estimate when she is due to re-surface.

On her next dive, I was commando style, crawling on the seaweed and stopping a few metres from the shoreline (close enough!). Luckily the wind direction was in my favour so

she did not get my scent. Finally she surfaced virtually in front of me, so close that I could hear her blowing down her nose, clearing her water away. I felt my heart pounding in my chest with excitement as down she went again, this time surfacing with a fish which she started to consume with a noisy munching sound as if relishing every chew. I laid as flat as I could watching every movement, almost forgetting that I had a camera with me. I started snapping away and she dived again this time popping up a little further along slowly making her way around the harbour and finally moving out of site. A good time now to move myself as she was unaware of my presence and I wanted to keep it that way. The last thing I wanted was to harass a wild animal.

I climbed up on to some nearby rocks and carefully peered over to see her once again fishing. I was not as close but still had great views of her zooming in through the lens. I could see that she had distinctive markings around her top lip giving her the appearance of having a moustache so we nicknamed her "Tasha". Then looking through the viewfinder there appeared a shot of Tasha staring back, I had been rumbled. I lay as still as possible as she gave me the once over but seemed not to be concerned and soon carried on fishing and swimming around the bay. I felt that she had been tolerant of me for long enough and left her in peace to carry on her daily life now seemingly on her own for by now her cubs must have started a new life on their own. We found "Tasha" on boxing day and spent three days watching her. It was a real treat and a nice Christmas present. Hopefully we will see her in the future as she appears to be a fit and healthy otter.

One day we had a trip down to Glenbrittle beach, one of our favourite spots.
As the road winds its way slowly down to the Cuillin mountains we get fantastic views of them from the car. Although impressive from a distance these mountains are truly awesome when viewed closely. They dominate the landscape and we struggle to see their tops from inside the car. A few miles further on we arrive at the car park at Glenbrittle beach followed shortly after by two beautiful large camper vans. We began chatting to the occupants who came from the far south of England and had travelled over eight hundred miles to get to Skye. They were staying for Christmas and New Year and their vans contained every home comfort imaginable including fridge, toilet, shower, television and even central heating. One van had three dogs on board and the other had two caged parrots, one of which could make dog barking noises and the other meowed like a cat. I suppose, at this time of year, it was a good job they could not do turkey impressions.

Walking on the beach a short while later we saw some oyster catches. These birds seem to be affected by a secret barrier because when you try to get a little closer to take photographs they start moving - but just enough to keep the same distance away, acting like repelling ends of two magnets.

Also on the beach and less shy are the hooded crows who are obviously quite intelligent birds. They search for mussels and shellfish which they clamp into their beaks before flying quite high and dropping them to the ground. On impact the shells are forced slightly open enabling the crows to get to their tasty snacks. If it is not too windy you can hear the sound of shells hitting the shore from various directions.

Boxing day night was not a night for much sleep as the weather forecast predicted storm warnings and they were not wrong. In the early hours it sounded as if the roof was coming off but by breakfast time the storm had moved away leaving behind an almost pleasant winters day. We decided to head north just beyond Dunvegan castle to Loch Suardal which is a place to see whooper swans. Although not a big stretch of water it does contain two or three families of whoopers as well as few golden eye ducks.

We watched the birds for about an hour and on our way back to the car, a small flock of ducks flashed passed us and disappeared into an adjoining stretch of water which was covered with tall reeds. Turning around we saw what had spooked them as coming up over the woods behind the loch was the unmistakable shape of a pair of golden eagles who effortlessly soared up on the wind and quickly disappeared from our viewpoint.

After arriving back at the car and loading the gear away we saw the ducks returning to their watery home after deciding between them that the coast was clear.

Unfortunately another Christmas week on Skye was over and we were heading back to our normal busy working lives, leaving Tasha the otter behind to carry on her normal wild existence. Hopefully we will see her again with a couple of new successful healthy cubs.

Winter Reflection - Loch Harport

Kilt Rock

Skye is a magical, timeless place. It can be moody and wild so much so that I have even seen waterfalls being blown backwards. But on a good day it is breathtakingly beautiful with all its rugged charm and once this island gets into your heart it will never leave.

## Timeless Landscape

Island misty dawn and heathery dew

Big skies abound with a heavenly view

Your shores lashed by countless storms

A landscape made taking numerous forms

Trees sculptured using natures hand

Glorious wilderness in a timeless land

To sit in quiet silence lost in time

As an otter stares back through seaweed and brine

Why these islands are thoughts every day

Even with these words it is still hard to say

————

Chris Banks

# Isle of Mull

## A Wildlife Haven

The island of Mull is a beautiful Hebridean island and has one of the most varied landscapes in Britain. It is wild, mountainous and has a coastline of approximately three hundred miles. It is another timeless landscape as well as being one of the major hot spots for all kinds of wildlife.

Wildlife camera man Gordon Buchanan, made a wonderful film about Mull which captures the island throughout the different seasons.

You can reach Mull by the main Ferry route from Oban, which is a journey of approximately forty-five minutes. Alternatively if you are on the Ardnamurchan peninsula there are shorter routes on smaller car ferries.

Chris & June - Carsaig Bay

Loch na Keal

Our first stay on Mull was with our friends, where we stayed in a lovely cottage at the very foot of Ben More (Mulls only Munro mountain).  As you drive to the cottage along Loch na Keal you see rocky outcrops, at various points, breaking through the surface of the water, which are usually occupied by lazing seals and occasionally the "White Tail Sea Eagle".

At the bottom of the drive to the cottage there is a small wooden chalet which just sleeps two. There is log burning stove and an open balcony bedroom, which is reached by a ladder (good fun). We have stayed here for a number of years and is affectionately know as "Wendy". This place has one of the finest views of the loch and is well positioned to witness fantastic sunsets, the colours of which can vary each night.

Directly behind the chalet is the dominating mass of Ben More and being on its doorstep it was only a matter of time before we headed up its lofty heights. The day we chose was a mix bag of weather, broken cloud and the odd shower.
The standard ascent route starts at the loch side at Dhiseig and leads you up beside the chalet. A little clue is given by the metal sign with an arrow and the word "UP".

Sunset over Loch na Keal

The walk is nothing too technical just a long slog upwards. When we reached halfway, we could see through the broken cloud, teasing views of small lochs and islands. But above us thicker cloud was moving in and the wind was starting to get stronger. We carried on with caution. A short while later the cloud really came down and visibility was about fifty yards. We sought shelter behind a large rock, had a drink of coffee and a sandwich, and thought about heading back down. On checking the altimeter

Ben More from the Isle of Ulva

on the watch we realised that we had only a few hundred feet to go, so we carried on. Eventually on reaching the summit it was howling a right old gale, with driving rain,  so hard that it was forcing the waterproofing out of my jacket, conditions the like of which we had never before experienced. There is usually a great feeling on reaching the summit of a mountain and a reluctance to head down, but not on this occasion.

Even on such a demanding day there were bonuses. A short while later we heard the distinctive call of the golden eagle, as well as seeing a mountain hare running directly in front of us. I suspect that he was surprised to see anybody on the mountain that day. Approaching the final leg of this journey was the welcoming sight of "Wendy". It was a great feeling to walk off the mountain directly into the chalet, having a hot shower and then relaxing next to a roaring log fire. We could not have been any wetter if we had fallen in the loch.

# Ulva

Try to find the time to visit the neighbouring island of Ulva as it is a great place to explore. There are no cars so access is as a foot passenger on a little boat that holds about twelve people and only takes a minute to cross. You attract the attention of the ferryman by sliding a red marker back on a board situated at the side of the jetty. This reveals a square that signals that you want to cross.

At the same point where you catch this ferry there are sometimes other boats waiting to take sightseers to other island groups such as the Treshnish isles.

The amusing thing is that these boats contain signs that state very clearly that they are not the Ulva ferry. Presumably they must have been asked many times. With my sense of humour I could just imagine one of these signs on the QE2.

Donald Munro - Ferryman

There are under thirty people
living on Ulva. We found one
small cafe and a cottage
displaying historical information.
There are various signposts
showing walks leading in all
directions, and you can wander
more or less where you like.
There has been recorded over a
hundred species of birds, such
as golden eagles and
corncrakes. The opportunity is
there to spot other types of
wildlife such as the red deer
and not forgetting those ever
elusive otters.

Woodland on Ulva

Water Mill

View from the Water

One of the walks takes you to the abandoned village of "Ormaig" with it collection of collapsed stone walls and stubborn gable ends that always seem to refuse to give in to time. A little further on you reach the ruin of a water mill complete with grinding stones. Life would have been hard when these buildings were occupied, but now there is a sense of sadness. I just wonder if they ever had the time to appreciate the magnificent views across to "Staffa" and the "Treshnish" isles, as we were appreciating them today.

This island has loads of history, and it is assured, that whichever walk you decide to take in this unspoiled emptiness, you will be in for a quiet day, and that one visit will not be enough.

Ormaig Village

Ormaig Village

Treshnish Isles

# Boat Trip

Travel north up to the islands capital Tobermory. The harbour front buildings are all painted in different colours, each seemingly vying for your attention. The air is sometimes filled with a distinctive smell of malt from Mulls only distillery.
The harbour is picturesque and filled with a myriad of boats of all different shapes and sizes from fishing trawlers to pleasure crafts and the odd old sailing boat.
Some  offer trips out into the Sound of Mull looking for whales, basking sharks, dolphins, and the smaller porpoises.
We decided that the sailing boat trip with wind power appealed to us.

Tobermory Harbour

On the morning of the trip, the weather was perfect, not a cloud in the sky and it was warm for a September day. We boarded around mid-day and first set off under engine power. By the time we reached open water the engine was cut and the sails were set. It is an eerie experience to be drifting along in silence, just listening to the waves and the sails flapping in the wind. Unfortunately we did not see any whales or dolphins but we did have encounters with the smaller porpoises, but again it is the anticipation of what you might just see that makes it exciting. The journey lasted about five hours and as we returned to the harbour it was a nice to see "Tobermory" in the early evening sunlight and from a different perspective.

Another trip we had was around the Treshnish Isles but this time we were in a smaller but more powerful boat. This time we did get close to a pair of basking sharks. Although they were bigger than the boat we felt quite at ease with these gentle giants. Having seen them on many wildlife documentaries it was a great thrill to see them for real.

Mull, like Skye, can have its magical
moments, whether it is with its
wildlife or its
natural, beautiful landscapes. Being
an amateur astronomer, the night
skies are truly amazing with so
many more stars visible to the
naked eye as a result of being away
from light pollution and orange
street lamps. One thing that stands
out is the "Milky Way" (This is the
centre section of our galaxy, as our
sun and planets, including the earth,
are on the outer reaches of one of
the spiral arms) which is normally
just visible on a clear night away
from city lights but on these
Scottish islands it is visible right
down to the horizon providing, of
course, that there is no moon.

# Wildlife on Mull

**Vole:** Wildlife on these islands comes in all shapes and sizes, some quiet easy to see, some requiring patience and a degree of luck. An example of the easy, was seen from our kitchen window in the chalet. There is a small raised lawn garden where we spread a little bread and peanuts out. You can watch the birds feeding along with the mice, shrew and the funniest of all, the voles, which appear to have a wind up clockwork mechanism. They run out from beneath the cover of vegetation, grab a piece of bread and zoom back at a speed which is difficult to believe.

**Mink:** One character we came across was the wild mink, which is not a native animal to our shores. They are escapees from breeding farms. This one was running along the bottom of Tobermory harbour wall at low tide. He was flitting in and out of the large gaps in the stone blocks and poking his head out from under the seaweed. Minks are vicious little killers and are trapped and caught as often as possible because they prove a threat to our native wildlife. But to look at our cheeky chap, who we named "MinkyMory", you would think that butter would not melt in his mouth.

**Otters:** The more elusive wildlife such as the otters can test your patience to the limit. One tip is to talk to people and find out and where the local hotspots are and where regular sightings occur. A word of warning, this does not mean that sightings are guaranteed, as a few years ago we had a whole week on Mull and did not see one otter.

### Otter

Elusive creatures we have watched on screen

To glimpse you for real the ultimate dream

Pulses racing with a telltale wake

The cursed mink a common mistake

A heartbeat missed this time its real

Mum and her cubs now earning their meal

Priceless views that are etched in our mind

A landscape with otters, but still hard to find

———

Chris Banks

On our most recent visit, our first encounter was within one hour of leaving the ferry when we were lucky enough to watch a mother otter and her two cubs frolicking in the bay. Returning to the same spot the next day we were sitting on the shore looking out for the otters when it started to rain heavily. Despite wearing camouflage clothing, the only thing to keep the camera dry was a bright red umbrella. Then to our astonishment right in front of us

we saw an otter head looking back at us through the seaweed. Feeling exited and privileged I managed to photograph her.
We thought we had seen the last of her, when, to our astonishment, she climbed out of the water and over the rocks and now it was our turn to be watched. I managed to photograph her again before she went back in to the water. By now we were soaked to the skin but it didn't matter, as her presence is now permanently etched in our minds.

**Sea Eagle:** Mull like Skye is home to a good many pairs of the magnificent "White Tail Seal Eagle" and also the more shy "Golden Eagles". Many nests are known around Mull and the chance  to see these birds flying is very high.
The sea eagles are sometimes know as lazy birds because when they are not feeding they can sit for hours, usually in their favourite tree, or perched on a well visited rock.
These birds are now making a comeback after their reintroduction in the seventies, but sadly not every year is a success with the new chicks, as accidents with nests do happen. Extreme weather conditions are often the cause. The birds are monitored and tagged regularly and wardens tour the known nesting sights to try and keep the birds protected which gives them every chance for success.

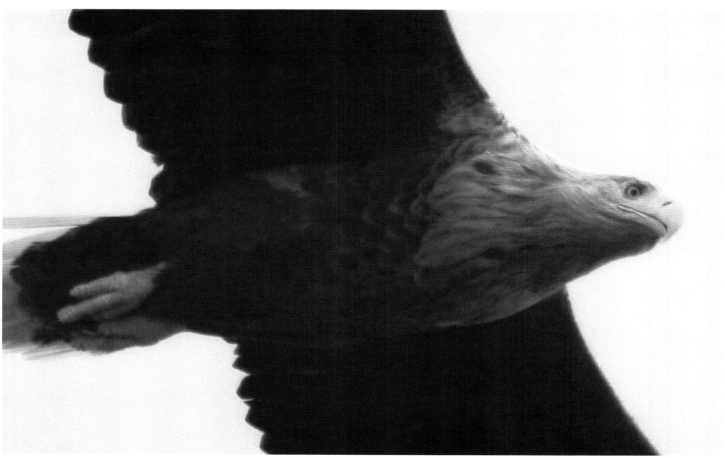

Loch Scridain

We witnessed a rare event whilst watching a large dog otter on Loch Scridain. We had been a few days observing this otter who turned out to be a real character and who we nicknamed him "Scriddy". He liked nothing more than, when out of the water, to be on his back with his feet in the air. After scouting round his normal hangouts we located him curled up asleep on a small rocky outcrop. He woke and started to fish so we followed him down the loch through our binoculars and could not believe what he did next. A

cormorant was swimming by when the otter came up from underneath and drowned the bird, then dragging his catch, he reached the shore where he began to eat his hard earned meal. He must have been one hungry otter. I am sure he was aware of my presence but was so intent on his meal that I was able to get a little closer without disturbing him. A wildlife tour bus had just pulled up and also witnessed the event. The tour guide mentioned he had been doing this job for twenty years and had never seen this happen before. He told us the otters have had small ducks but nothing as large as a cormorant. And though not pleasant to witness, you have to accept that this is wildlife in the raw, and this is part of their survival.

### Mull

An Island sanctuary un-molested by time

A banquet for the senses you will never find on line

Car journeys broken with possible encounters

Eagle or Otter, or just views that enchant us

Coloured sunsets with soft pastel glows

No filter required one of natures natural shows

An Island of memories no fear of being full

A place of mystery? No!   it's simply called "Mull"

————

Chris Banks

# Salen Boats

A familiar landmark at Salen, for many years is three wrecked fishing boats which lay abandoned to the elements. There are many similar sights as you travel around Mull but these must be the most famous and the most photographed. Just about every time you pass you see that someone has stopped and is snapping away from every possible angle. When you find yourself at these boats alone it always feels a quiet and peaceful location. Many is the time we have stopped for our lunch here when we have been on our travels. It is like eating with old friends. The scene changes regularly depending on the tides, although at low tide there is a feeling of sadness as the boats can be seen emptying the sea water from their rotten hulls.

I am sure that if these boats could talk, there would be many tales of hard work and happier times. But now they are ending their days together sharing a well known visitors spot. It is also a great place to see otters as there are regular sightings from this bay. Again it is not guaranteed but with luck and patience you should be rewarded with a view of these elusive creatures.

Unfortunately this well known spot may be changed for ever as there are rumours of plans to modernise the roadway to Tobermory and the old boats may have to be moved. Hopefully the otters will quickly adapt to their changed surroundings.

### Elsie May

Huddled together in a small sheltered bay

Fishing no more now old "Elsie May"

Strange faces turning that stop and stare

Rotten wooden hulls with souls laid bare

A local landmark with visitors bound

These familiar friends now sleeping sound

Suffering storms and waves to fend

Now part of the landscape a dignified end

Chris Banks

Salen Boats

Reluctantly we have to leave these timeless landscapes. The empty, silent lochs and glens and the deserted mountains will always be remembered - as will the rare and unexpected wildlife encounters. Plans will certainly be made for our next trip to this beautiful area.

On our return home, after unpacking and cleaning the car, the following thought always comes to mind:-

**"You can wash the Islands out of your car,
but you cannot wash the Islands out of your soul"**